Little People, **BIG DREAMS**

ELTON JOHN

Written by
Maria Isabel Sánchez Vegara

Illustrated by
Sophie Beer

Frances Lincoln
Children's Books

This is the story of a little boy from the London suburbs, who once sat at the piano and started playing a waltz by ear. His name was Reggie, and from that day on, whenever his parents argued, music became his refuge.

He received a scholarship to study classical music at the Royal Academy of Music. By singing in the choir and playing with other musicians, he discovered what music is all about: bringing people together.

Reggie started composing his own melodies and singing
rock and roll hits with a band. One day, he saw an advert
from a record company, looking for new talent . . .
He decided to go to the audition.

Reggie didn't do very well that day. Still, he left the try-out with an envelope full of lyrics from a guy called Bernie that all needed a melody. Back home, when Reggie started reading . . . something magical happened!

Reggie wasn't the best at writing lyrics, and Bernie didn't know how to write melodies. But by working together, all they needed was 15 minutes to make the most beautiful songs.

After two long years of composing songs for other artists, it was time for Reggie to record his first solo album. But Reginald Kenneth wasn't the coolest name for an artist, so he changed it to Elton John.

One morning, Elton and Bernie wrote a song at breakfast. It was called "Your Song" and it launched Elton like a rocket man, from his mother's modest house to superstardom! It was his first big hit.

Jumping on stage dressed as Captain Fantastic, Elton became a celebrity loved by millions. He had thousands of spectacular glasses and the most amazing wardrobe a drag queen would long for.

But once the show was over and the adoring crowds had left, Elton felt terribly alone. He had all he could dream of, and still, nothing seemed to make him happy.

Everything changed when he met Ryan, a little hero fighting in hospital. Ryan showed him that life's too wonderful to waste it complaining. The day they said goodbye, Elton promised to honor his friend's memory by being his best self.

And he did! He started eating healthily, getting a good night's sleep, and looking after himself. And then came David, the husband he had always wanted. They built their own family and are the proud fathers of two children.

Elton was knighted by the Queen of England, not just for being the most successful male solo artist of all time, but also for creating a fantastic foundation to fight AIDS, the disease that had taken Ryan and many other friends away.

And after a long life dedicated to music, Sir Elton John still remembers little Reggie. The shy boy who looked for comfort sitting at his piano, and ended up bringing joy and happiness to the world with his songs.

ELTON JOHN

(Born 1947)

1968

1973

Reginald Kenneth Dwight was born in Middlesex, England, in 1947. Inspired by musical greats like Little Richard and Ray Charles, Reggie taught himself to play piano. His father disagreed with Reggie's dream of pop super-stardom, but Reggie didn't let that stop him. At the age of 17, he realized he wanted to transform himself, so he borrowed two of his bandmates' names, and Elton John was born. In 1967, Elton met Bernie Taupin, and together the duo wrote hits that no one could predict: pop-ballads like "Your Song," rock and roll dance-alongs like "Crocodile Rock," and sing-at-the-top-of-your-voice anthems like "I'm Still Standing." On stage, Elton could be anything he dreamed, and the crowds loved him for it. He could make you sing, dance, laugh, and cry. When he pulled his signature move on stage—

1971

2014

a handstand on his piano—it felt like the whole room was floating up
with him. Elton also became known for some crazy outfits, full of feathers,
pompoms, sequins, and sunglasses you had to see to believe. His wildest
dreams had come true—why not dress for the occasion? Elton has had 27
top 10 hits, won countless awards, and even performed at Queen Elizabeth
II's Diamond Jubilee! He was knighted in 1998 for his music and charity work
with the Elton John AIDS Foundation, which Elton set up in memory of his
friend, Ryan White. In 2018, he announced he would quit touring to spend
more time with his husband and two kids. He remains one of the world's best-
loved singers and an LGBTQ+ icon, the boy from Middlesex who dreamed
big, and became everyone's favorite Rocket Man.

Want to find out more about **Elton John?**

Have a read of these great books:

Who Is Elton John? by Kirsten Anderson and Joseph J. M. Qiu

The Lion King: Piano/Vocal (Sheet Music) by Elton John and Tim Rice

Q Quarto Knows

Inspiring | Educating | Creating | Entertaining

Brimming with creative inspiration, how-to projects, and useful information to enrich your everyday life, Quarto Knows is a favourite destination for those pursuing their interests and passions. Visit our site and dig deeper with our books into your area of interest: Quarto Creates, Quarto Cooks, Quarto Homes, Quarto Lives, Quarto Drives, Quarto Explores, Quarto Gifts, or Quarto Kids.

Concept and text © 2020 Maria Isabel Sánchez Vegara. Illustrations © 2020 Sophie Beer

First Published in the US in 2020 by Frances Lincoln Children's Books, an imprint of The Quarto Group.

Quarto Boston North Shore, 100 Cummings Center, Suite 265D, Beverly, MA 01915, USA

Tel: +1 978-282-9590, Fax: +1 978-283-2742 **www.QuartoKnows.com**

First Published in Spain in 2020 under the title Pequeño & Grande Elton John

by Alba Editorial, s.l.u., Baixada de Sant Miquel, 1, 08002 Barcelona

www.albaeditorial.es

All rights reserved.

Published by arrangement with Alba Editorial, s.l.u. Translation rights arranged by IMC Agència Literària, SL

All rights reserved.

A catalogue record for this book is available from the British Library.

ISBN 978-0-7112-5840-2

Set in Futura BT.

Published by Katie Cotton • Designed by Sasha Moxon

Edited by Katy Flint • Editorial Assistance from Alex Hithersay

Production by Nikki Ingram

Manufactured in Guangdong, China CC082020

1 3 5 7 9 8 6 4 2

Photographic acknowledgements (pages 28-29, from left to right) 1. Photo of Elton JOHN; First publicity pictures - in Hampstead (Photo by Val Wilmer/Redferns) 2. English pop singer Elton John in a flamboyant stage outfit of feather trimmed jacket and rhinestone encrusted glasses, circa 1973. (Photo by Terry O'Neill/Iconic Images/Getty Images) 3. English singer songwriter Elton John performing at Dodger Stadium in Los Angeles, 1975. He is wearing a sequinned baseball outfit. (Photo by Terry O'Neill/Iconic Images/Getty Images) 4. Elton John performs live at Twickenham Stoop on June 3, 2017 in London, England. (Photo by Ian Gavan/Getty Images for Harlequins)

Collect the
Little People, BIG DREAMS series:

FRIDA KAHLO

ISBN: 978-1-84780-783-0

COCO CHANEL

ISBN: 978-1-84780-784-7

MAYA ANGELOU

ISBN: 978-1-84780-889-9

AMELIA EARHART

ISBN: 978-1-84780-888-2

AGATHA CHRISTIE

ISBN: 978-1-84780-960-5

MARIE CURIE

ISBN: 978-1-84780-962-9

ROSA PARKS

ISBN: 978-1-78603-018-4

AUDREY HEPBURN

ISBN: 978-1-78603-053-5

EMMELINE PANKHURST

ISBN: 978-1-78603-020-7

ELLA FITZGERALD

ISBN: 978-1-78603-087-0

ADA LOVELACE

ISBN: 978-1-78603-076-4

JANE AUSTEN

ISBN: 978-1-78603-120-4

GEORGIA O'KEEFFE

ISBN: 978-1-78603-122-8

HARRIET TUBMAN

ISBN: 978-1-78603-227-0

ANNE FRANK

ISBN: 978-1-78603-229-4

MOTHER TERESA

ISBN: 978-1-78603-230-0

JOSEPHINE BAKER

ISBN: 978-1-78603-228-7

L. M. MONTGOMERY

ISBN: 978-1-78603-233-1

JANE GOODALL

ISBN: 978-1-78603-231-7

SIMONE DE BEAUVOIR

ISBN: 978-1-78603-232-4

MUHAMMAD ALI

ISBN: 978-1-78603-331-4

STEPHEN HAWKING

ISBN: 978-1-78603-333-8

MARIA MONTESSORI

ISBN: 978-1-78603-755-8

VIVIENNE WESTWOOD

ISBN: 978-1-78603-757-2

MAHATMA GANDHI
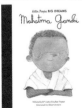
ISBN: 978-1-78603-787-9

DAVID BOWIE

ISBN: 978-1-78603-332-1

WILMA RUDOLPH

ISBN: 978-1-78603-751-0

DOLLY PARTON

ISBN: 978-1-78603-760-2

BRUCE LEE

ISBN: 978-1-78603-789-3

RUDOLF NUREYEV

ISBN: 978-1-78603-791-6

ZAHA HADID

ISBN: 978-1-78603-745-9

MARY SHELLEY

ISBN: 978-1-78603-748-0

MARTIN LUTHER KING JR.
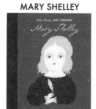
ISBN: 978-0-7112-4567-9

DAVID ATTENBOROUGH

ISBN: 978-0-7112-4564-8

ASTRID LINDGREN

ISBN: 978-0-7112-5217-2

EVONNE GOOLAGONG

ISBN: 978-0-7112-4586-0

BOB DYLAN

ISBN: 978-0-7112-4675-1

ALAN TURING

ISBN: 978-0-7112-4678-2

BILLIE JEAN KING
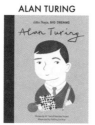
ISBN: 978-0-7112-4693-5

GRETA THUNBERG

ISBN: 978-0-7112-5645-3

JESSE OWENS

ISBN: 978-0-7112-4583-9

JEAN-MICHEL BASQUIAT

ISBN: 978-0-7112-4580-8

ARETHA FRANKLIN

ISBN: 978-0-7112-4686-7

CORAZON AQUINO

ISBN: 978-0-7112-4684-3

PELÉ

ISBN: 978-0-7112-4573-0

ERNEST SHACKLETON

ISBN: 978-0-7112-4571-6

STEVE JOBS

ISBN: 978-0-7112-4577-8

AYRTON SENNA

ISBN: 978-0-7112-4672-0

LOUISE BOURGEOIS

ISBN: 978-0-7112-4690-4

ELTON JOHN

ISBN: 978-0-7112-5840-2